From Devon With Love

From Devon With Love

An evocative view of Devon photographed by BOB CROXFORD

See that ye hold fast the Heritage we leave you
Yea and teach your children the value that may fail them, or their hands grow weak.

SIR FRANCIS DRAKE

Published by ATMOSPHERE

To Tony Colmer ~ Lost at sea 1994
"For some, the cost of fish is too high"

FROM DEVON WITH LOVE

Photographs copyright Bob Croxford 1994
Text copyright Bob Croxford 1994
(Except where separately acknowledged)

First published by ATMOSPHERE in 1994
Willis Vean
Mullion
Helston Cornwall TR12 7DF
TEL:01326-240180
FAX:01326-240900

ISBN 0 9521850 1 6

Designed by Butcher Murray Skyner
Origination in the West Country by Scantec
Printed in the West Country by Lawrence Allen
Printed in England

Also published by ATMOSPHERE

FROM CORNWALL WITH LOVE

ISBN 0 9521850 0 8

COVER PICTURE : Buckland in the Moor
BACKGROUND : Reflections in South Devon

CONTENTS

INTRODUCTION

I remember a visit to Devon years ago. It was during a London heat-wave. Jenny and I escaped to the country. We spent a long weekend, stopping at B&Bs where we could. At the end of a sultry afternoon we arrived at Clovelly. Pulling into the car park, we were just in time to see the last coach, full of trippers, leaving the car park. We spent a couple of hours exploring the village. The two of us were the only visitors. The pub half-way down the hill provided accommodation. The next morning the sun woke us early. We spent some time sitting on the harbour wall before a leisurely breakfast. We walked slowly back up the hill to our car. As we left the car park the first tour bus was arriving.

In the height of summer we had enjoyed Clovelly, as its only visitors. Even today, if you arrive late and leave early, Devon can still be enjoyed in timeless beauty.

Devon has meant many different things to me. While a teenage learner driver I remember a family holiday in Torbay. (At least my hill starts were good!) When re-directing my career as a landscape photographer it was in Devon that I received much encouragement. Now that I visit the county several times a year, I have come to know it well.

My routes through Devon are numerous and varied. I have favourite views which can be visited over and over again. On each visit the weather and the season have changed. The scenery becomes fresh each time.

Contrasts in Devon are many. From the wilderness of Dartmoor to the sheltered estuaries of South Hams, from the dramatic cliffs of the north coast to ancient towns like Exeter. All the facets make a truly interesting county. Only the total is Devon but many of the parts are unique.

The long swathe of farmland between Barnstaple and Seaton has mile after mile of green rolling fields. Certainly, a few large roads intrude but most of the area is accessible only by a network of narrow lanes. From the brow of each hill you see yet more well-tended fields lined with ancient hedgerows. In spring, with fields in different stages of planting and growing, one can drive, or walk, for hours through a patchwork of green. This undulating landscape is everyone's idea of perfect English scenery.

This book does not try to be a guide-book. Nor is it a comprehensive survey or history. Instead it is a collection of photographs which added together evoke a feel or taste of this varied county. No single image can say all there is about a place. Perhaps several pictures can create a true impression.

The anthology of Devon writing, which accompanies the pictures, is an eclectic collection. It includes both the ancient and the contemporary. In the selection of the pieces I have followed the same idea as the photographs. No piece, on its own, will tell more than a fragment. Taken together an evocation of this rich and varied county will hopefully emerge. This is not an illustrated anthology. The words are intended as a counterpoint to the images, not as captions.

The county was at the centre of historic events in the 15th,

16th and 17th Centuries. There were many writers who recorded what they experienced around them. A very distinct kind of hero hailed from Devon in those days. Ralegh, Drake and Hawkins were famous in the Elizabethan era of swashbuckling and derring-do. When one reads accounts of travel through Devon in those times, largely on muddy horse and pack-mule tracks, it is not surprising that these men went to sea. Likewise, much of the writing, from this time, concerns the sea.

The railways put the county within easier reach of London. A different type of writer now makes an appearance, sometimes on holiday. Writers like Keats, Kipling, Dickens and Browning were either enchanted or appalled at the difference between Devon and London.

Animals seem to feature frequently in Devon stories. The Hound of the Baskervilles and Tarka the Otter are probably the best known. My own impression is that the animal book authors are amongst the most creative of writers. Henry Williamson, David Rook and Brian Carter have written descriptive prose of rare insight.

With such an historic past, it is not surprising that romantic novelists have been attracted to set their books in Devon.

In the sixties and seventies Devon came under a different spotlight. This was the period when the county was developing mass tourism. The attractions of Devon's scenery brought film and television crews to the county.

Before looking at Devon to make photographs I am influenced by the history and creativity that has gone before. Much is intangible and fragile. I hope that what I have found is still there, in years to come, for others to discover.

*S*ometimes a moment from the past comes winging back and I shiver with thoughts of might-have-been. Then I look through my window on to the sands below, with the grey, thunderous Atlantic beyond and Lundy Island dim in the distance. The treacherous self-pity subsides. I know I made the right decision.

DANIEL FARSON

*T*he manner of producing clouted cream is as follows: The milk is strained into shallow pans, each containing about half-a-pint of water to prevent the milk from adhering to the sides. In these it is allowed to remain undisturbed for twelve or twenty-four hours, according to the weather. It is then scalded, and often in Devonshire farmhouses by a wood fire (which gives the butter made from it the smoky taste that some like and some dislike), or better, according to modern usage by warm water. In the former case it is moved slowly towards the fire so as to become gradually heated, and in about forty or fifty minutes the cream is formed. This is indicated by bubbles, and takes place at a temperature of 180° Fahrenheit. The milk is then removed from the fire, and skimmed from twelve to thirty-six hours afterwards.

JOHN M HAWKER   1881

<Deckchairs

Devon Cream Tea>

I ascended, with some toil, the highest point; two large stones inclining on each other formed a rude portal on the summit. Here I sat down. A little level platform, about two yards long, lay before me, and then the eye immediately fell upon the sea, far, very far below. I never felt the sublimity of solitude before.

ROBERT SOUTHEY   1799

*T*he peasantry of North Devon, as I have discovered for these two or three days past, are a very superior race to the labouring poor of the more eastern parts of the kingdom. Imbibing from the pure air of their native mountains mental vigour as well as corporal strength, they exhibit a sagacity and quickness which only require culture, to produce characters shining and energetic.

RICHARD WARNER   1800

Lynmouth Sunset >

< *Valley of the Rocks*

11

*M*y walk to Ilfracombe led me through Lynmouth, the finest spot,
except Cintra and the Arrabida, that I ever saw.

ROBERT SOUTHEY   1799

*A*t Lynmouth the destructive force of the river torrent was many
times greater still, for there it came down from rugged heights
immediately above the village, loosing on Lynmouth an avalanche of
giant boulders and great uprooted trees.

THE TIMES 18 AUGUST 1952

The Rising Sun, Lynmouth >

< Exmoor Wall

A stream flowed through the wood, moving lazily over a gravel bed with few rocks to impede its progress. In the shallows, where the stream changed its course, patches of fragrant meadowsweet swayed gently, while rich purple masses of loosestrife seemed to glow in the shadow of the banks.

T he clear water was dancing with insect-life; pond-skaters and whirligig beetles made crazy patterns on the surface, while beneath the surface moved water-boatman, water-beetles and the countless larvae of a dozen different species; the sinister shape of a water-scorpion lurked in a tangle of weed, and dragon-fly larvae stalked the stream-bed like prehistoric tigers. Above the stream, mayflies dipped and shimmered on filigree wings, dimpling the surface where they brushed it and filling the luminous dusk with dancing motes of light.

DAVID ROOK   1974

<Watersmeet

Watersmeet>

*T*he people in Devonshire never swear, nor have I heard one speak ill
of another during almost 9 months I have lived in it.

JOHN GABRIEL STEDMAN   1744-1797

Yes, I delight, when winds and waters roar,
To tread with shrinking foot the craggy shore;
And watch each billow with collected force
Urge o'er the whirling sands its frothy course:
O'er yon black rock, whose frowning bastion braves
And breaks the onset of the wintry waves,
To mark it dash in snowy showers its spray
That flames and flashes in the blaze of day;
Or fall from ledge to ledge like mountain stream,
Its foam-balls reddened by the evening beam.

SIR AUBREY DE VERE   1850

Watermouth Bay >

< Ilfracombe

Every earth-picture thus depends upon the sky-picture spread over it, and when the sun is absent, the spacious diffusion of light effected by cloud and humid air will oftentimes beget luminous most beautiful conditions, will magnify unconsidered incident of landscape, and reveal chastened colour-harmonies that are lost in the more obvious magnificence of direct sunlight. And upon this, my silver day, the children of sunshine slept.

EDEN PHILLPOTTS   1904

<Croyde

Saunton Sands>

All who have travelled through the delicious scenery of North Devon, must needs know the little white town of Bideford, which slopes upwards from its broad tide-river paved with yellow sands, and many-arched old bridge where salmon wait for autumn floods, toward the pleasant upland on the west. Above the town the hills close in, cushioned with deep oak woods, through which juts here and there a crag of fern-fringed slate; below they lower, and open more and more in softly-rounded knolls, and fertile squares of red and green, till they sink into the wide expanse of hazy flats, rich salt marshes, and rolling sand-hills, where Torridge joins her sister Taw, and both together flow quietly toward the broad surges of the bar, and the everlasting thunder of the long Atlantic swell. Pleasantly the old town stands there, beneath its soft Italian sky, fanned day and night by the fresh ocean breeze, which forbids alike the keen winter frosts, and the fierce thunder heats of the midland; and pleasantly it has stood there for now, perhaps, eight hundred years, since the first Grenvile, cousin of the Conqueror, returning from the conquest of South Wales, drew round him trusty Saxon serfs, and free Norse rovers with their golden curls, and dark Silurian Britons from the Swansea shore, and all the mingled blood which still gives to the seaward folk of the next county their strength and intellect, and, even in these levelling days, their peculiar beauty of face and form.

CHARLES KINGSLEY 1855

From the nesse up to Bedeford bridge apon Turege a 4. miles, wher is a praty quik streat of smithes and other occupiers for ship crafte cis pontem. The bridge at Bedeford apon Turege is a very notable worke, and hath xxiiij. arches of stone, and is fairly waullid on eche side. But the arches be not so high as the arches of Berstaple bridge be. A poore preste began this bridge, and, as it is saide, he was animatid to do so by a vision. Then all the cuntery about sette their handes onto the performing of it: and sins landes hath be gyven to the maintenaunce of it.

< Bideford

Barnstaple >

JOHN LELAND C1540

The population of Clovelly is almost entirely seafaring: or rather, the men are fisherfolk, and the men's wives have for years past found a second string to the domestic bow in letting bedrooms and providing refreshments for visitors; so that when circumstances forbid the chase of the herring there is not likely to be that empty cupboard at home, which is apt to vex the lives and haunt the imaginations of the fisherfolk of most other seaboard places. What competition there is in this ministering to visitors is necessarily very limited, because Clovelly itself is unexpanding. What it was sixty or seventy years ago, that it remains in almost every detail to-day.

CHARLES G HARPER   1908

… And now, gentle readers, farewell; and farewell, Clovelly, and all the loving hearts it holds; and farewell, too, the soft still summer weather.

CHARLES KINGSLEY   1849

Clovelly Arch>

<Clovelly Harbour

"And a mighty sing'lar and pretty place it is, as ever I saw in all the days of my life!" said Captain Jorgan, looking up at it.

Captain Jorgan had to look high up at it, for the village was built sheer up the face of a steep and lofty cliff. There was no road in it, there was no wheeled vehicle in it, there was not a level yard in it. From the sea-beach to the cliff-top two irregular rows of white houses, placed opposite to one another, and twisting here and there, and there and here, rose, like the sides of a long succession of stages of crooked ladders, and you climbed up the village or climbed down the village by the staves between, some six feet wide or so, and made of sharp irregular stones. The old pack-saddle, long laid aside in most parts of England as one of the appendages of its infancy, flourished here intact. Strings of pack-horses and pack-donkeys toiled slowly up the staves of the ladders, bearing fish, and coal, and such other cargo as was unshipping at the pier from the dancing fleet of village boats and from two or three little coasting traders. As the beasts of burden ascended laden, or descended light, they so got lost at intervals in the floating clouds of village smoke, that they seemed to dive down some of the village chimneys, and come to the surface again afar off, high above others. No two houses in the village were alike, in chimney, size, shape, door, window, gable, roof-tree, anything. The sides of the ladders were musical with water, running clear and bright. The staves were musical with the clattering feet of the pack-horses and pack-donkeys, and the voices of the fishermen urging them up, mingled with the voices of the fishermen's wives and their many children.

CHARLES DICKENS AND WILKIE COLLINS   C 1880

*B*y pools and waterfalls and rillets the river Taw grew, flowing under steep hills that towered high above. It washed the roots of its first tree, a willow thin and sparse of bloom, a soft tree wildered in that place of rocks and rain and harsh grey harrying winds. A black-faced sheep stood by the tree, cropping the sweet grass; and when a strange, small, flashing, frightening head looked out just below its feet, the sheep stamped and bounded away up the hill to its lamb asleep by a sun-hot boulder. Tarka had caught a trout, the first in a mile of river; he ate it, drank, and slipped away with the water.

HENRY WILLIAMSON   1927

< Marsh Orchid

River Torridge >

Drake answered with a thoughtful look,

A calm, unruffled brow,

As up the bowl he gravely took,

And to his chief did bow;

"Whene'er the Spaniards come, my Lord,

We'll show them English sport,

But for the time can well afford

To keep our ships in port;

For we will follow in the track,

and bring the foe to bay,

Brave, trusty hearts we do not lack,

Who fear nor storm nor fray;

We'll teach the Dons how Britons fight,

On land or ocean deep,

So let us rest, my lord, to-night,

And watchful vigils keep."

W H K WRIGHT   1874

I was at Plymouth, and walking on the
Hoo, which is a plain on the edge of
the sea, looking to the road, I observed
the evening so serene, so calm, so
bright, and the sea so smooth, that a
finer sight, I think, I never saw.

DANIEL DEFOE   1704

Plymouth Hoe >

< Smeaton's Monument

THE SHIP

This year his friend Sir Joshua Reynolds paid a visit of some weeks to his native country, Devonshire, in which he was accompanied by Johnson, who was much pleased with this jaunt, and declared he had derived from it a great accession of new ideas. He was entertained at the seats of several noblemen and gentlemen in the West of England; but the greatest part of the time was passed at Plymouth, where the magnificence of the navy, the ship-building and all its circumstances, afforded him a grand subject of contemplation.

BOSWELL 1762

In GREAT GOOD SPIRITS the crew brought the ship into Plymouth Harbour, which is one of the ports of England. Anchor was dropped and Captain Fayerman struck the sails. Although the season was winter, and there was rain and snow, the distant view of the city looked like a paradise to rival the Garden of Eden. We saw a beautiful green field with trees to shame the palm-groves of paradise. Sweet-singing birds warbled the psalms of David and Christian melodies refreshed our souls. And by this beautiful field there rose a hill, high as the hopes of lovers, with graceful trees spaced no further apart than their height, their branches arm-in-arm like affectionate brothers.

MIRZA ABUL HASSAN KHAN   1809-10

< Plymouth

Plymouth >

Being agog to see some Devonshire, I would have taken a walk the first day, but the rain would not let me; and the second, but the rain would not let me; and the third, but the rain forbade it. Ditto 4 - ditto 5 - ditto - so I made up my mind to stop in-doors, and catch a sight flying between the showers: and, behold I saw a pretty valley - pretty cliffs, pretty Brooks, pretty Meadows, pretty trees, both standing as they were created, and blown down as they are uncreated. The green is beautiful, as they say, and pity it is that it is amphibious.

JOHN KEATS   1818

The lane of tall, white hawthorn hedges was hung here and there with dogroses. If he climbed the bank and pressed his face to the small pink flowers he could breathe their scent which was never very strong. Dogroses, hayfields, the distant cuckoo and a blue sky! God, he sighed to himself, is there a lovelier place or a lovelier season? Devon, the South Hams and the coombe.

BRIAN CARTER   1984

∧ *Bantham Boat House*

South Hams Estuary >

"The banks are so high to the left hand and right,
That they shut up the beauties around them from sight,
And hence you'll allow 'tis and inference plain
That marriage is just like a Devonshire lane."

ANON

Of this strong drink, much like to Stygian lake,
Most term it ale, I know not what to make,
Folk drink it thick, and piss it out full thin,
Much dregs therefore must needs remain within.

HENRY OF AVRANCHES   13TH CENTURY

< Modbury

Devon Wall >

...with an inner glow that enshrined the day's splendour. To the West, golden mists shone above the setting-place of the sun and already fashioned the glories of his pall; such rest and peace as only Autumn knows brooded over the world; and in the silence one could almost hear the downward flutter of each leaf, the fall of seed and gleaming berry, as they descended to the earth. Orchards and beechwoods, oakwoods, sere stubbles, and acres of ripe roots lay there in the glory of accomplishment. The harvest was complete, to the cup of the little campion brimming with grain beneath my eye; all had nobly ended, and the blessing of rest was well won.

EDEN PHILLPOTTS   1904

Hope Cove >

< *Thurlestone Rock*

The place nestles within a wide crescent of gentle hills that tend towards the sea, and shine at this season with ripening corn and bright red earth, with fresh green of root crops, and gentle bloom of summer forests that mark the undulations of the land. Near the western point of this semicircle the Start's white lighthouse stands, and eastward tall cliffs arise, from which the whole subtending scene is visible, and miles of glittering mere may be perceived in one glance of the eye. Here spreads a lake, so near the sea that the waves make their music to the tarn, and great reeds that fringe it return messages on the land breeze. Beaches of bright shingle, shining sands, and miles of flowers lie between the silver fresh water and the blue salt. Soft grey enfolds the scene on this day of Summer, and beneath a bright sky, wherein the light is diffused in an equable and pearly haze just slashed and fretted with blue like a fair sea-shell, this ley of reeds and lilies, together with its banks of verdure, the sands around, and the sea beyond, weave such a robe of wonderful colour for the earth as shall seldom adorn even summer hours.

EDEN PHILLPOTTS   1904

Slapton >

< Start Point Lighthouse

TO DEVONSHIRE

O, take me back to Devonshire
To glimpse again her green;
To see once more her winter grey,
Her leafy summer sheen.

O, take me back to Devonshire
To walk the lanes of June,
To listen to the bluebells
Trumpeting their tune.

O, take me back to Devonshire
To wander through the corn,
To sip the dew from buttercups
Unfolding to the dawn.

O, take me back to Devonshire
To stand in twilight hours,
A-dreaming in the fragrance
Of her gay laburnum bowers.

O, take me back to Devonshire
To live in quietude,
And I'll repay your kindliness
With tears of gratitude.

NOEL PATON S   1884

Salcombe >

< Beach at East Portlemouth

*Y*ou zee, now-a-days us gets scores and hundreds o' visitors to Muddlecombe, one time and another. I can mind the time, and not so very long agone neether, when if a stranger went droo the village all the parrish would be out to look at'n, and discuss who he was and where he come from and where he was gwain to and what he was on upon. But now, bless yer 'art, with so many o' the ole cherrybims coming out from the gurt towns, 'tis nothing onusual to zee as much as thirty or vowerty strange volks in the strate, all to once. And very off'n they comes from plaaces right up-the-contry which us never yeard of bevore. 'Tis wonderful the distance they ole cherrybims will travel.

JAN STEWER   1925

< *Salcombe*

South Hams Boathouse >

*M*r Isaac Pointz removed a cigar from his lips and said approvingly:
"Pretty little place."

Having thus set the seal of his approval upon Dartmouth harbour, he
replaced the cigar and looked about him with the air of a man pleased
with himself, his appearance, his surroundings and life generally.

AGATHA CHRISTIE   1939

< Dartmouth

Bayard's Quay >

My dear Forster,

I took a cottage for them this morning. If they are not pleased with it - I shall be grievously disappointed, that's all. It is at a place called Alphington, exactly one mile beyond Exeter on the Dawlish, I think, but I know on the Plymouth road. There are two white cottages together, built of brick with thatched roofs. One is theirs and the other belongs to their landlady one Mrs Pannell. I almost forget the number of rooms and cannot say positively until I have been there again, but I can report on solemn affirmation that on the ground floor there are an excellent parlour, a nice kitchen, and a little third room of comfortable proportions; and that in the yard behind there are meat safes, cellars, coal holes, wood houses, and such like accommodations in rural abundance. Upstairs there is really a beautiful little room over the parlour which I am furnishing as a drawing-room, and I am not sure whether there are two or three bedrooms besides. There is a splendid garden and the rent of the whole (the landlady paying all taxes) is twenty pounds a year! The paint and paper throughout is new and fresh and cheerful-looking: the place is clean beyond all description; and the neighbourhood I suppose the most beautiful in this most beautiful of English counties.

Mrs Pannell, of whom I must make most especial mention, is a Devonshire widow with whom I had the honour of taking lunch today. She is a fat, infirm, splendidly-fresh-faced country dame, rising sixty and recovering from an attack "on the nerves"- I thought they never went off the stones, but I find they try country air with the best of us.

CHARLES DICKENS   1839

*T*otnes is about the size of Mullingar, but busier, wealthier, and much more lively. Apart from the quiet hurry of market day, gentleness is the first quality to give it; gentleness in its buildings, and in the coming and going of its people; and in the slow, winding, winding of the River Dart from the moor to the sea. Oh, lord, the natural lie of it is lovely. Except when visitors pour in during the brief summer, the town is so quiet that it looks like a grey-haired lady, with a young face, sitting calm, hands in lap, unmindful of time, in an orchard of ageing trees, drowsy with the scent of ripened apples about to fall, but which never do;

SEAN O'CASEY   1880 - 1964

Totnes >

< Hope Cottages

THE WIVES OF BRIXHAM

You see the gentle water,
How silently it floats,
How cautiously, how steadily
It moves the sleepy boats;
And all the little loops of pearl
It strews along the sand
Steal out as leisurely as leaves,
When summer is at hand.

The merry boats of Brixham
Go out to search the seas,
A fleet all staunch and sturdy,
Who love a swinging breeze;
And off the woods of Devon,
Or silvery cliffs of Wales,
Is seen on summer evenings
The light upon their sails.

ANON   1880'S

I enjoyed a glorious fortnight in
Torquay at the height of the summer
season, but never ventured to
neighbouring Paignton where it was
rumoured there were signs excluding
dogs and sailors from the town's parks!

E V THOMPSON   1986

< Brixham Night

Brixham >

The pishgies or pixies of Devon are brothers to the Gaelic shidhe.
They do the same curious things- stealing babies from cradles and leaving changelings in their place; misleading travellers in the dark; galloping wildly about on the moorland ponies, a minor manner of the Irish pooka. At time they do good things, threshing a farmer's corn for him; but they must be watched, and food, fresh and tasty, must be left for them on the farmhouse floor.

SEAN O'CASEY   1954

.......No wonder that such a spot as Torquay with its delicious Italian climate, and endless variety of rich woodland, flowery lawn, fantastic rock-cavern, and broad bright tide-sand, sheltered from every wind of heaven except the soft south-east, should have become a favourite haunt, not only for invalids, but for naturalists.

CHARLES KINGSLEY 1855

< *South Devon Landscapes*

Cockington >

50

I am better, you see - and thankful for being so, on one account (as far as concerns myself) for it gives me hope that they will soon let me go away from this dreadful dreadful place.

ELIZABETH BARRET BROWNING   1840

The spring of '96 saw us in Torquay, where we found a house for our heads that seemed almost too good to be true. It was large and bright, with big rooms each and all open to the sun, the grounds embellished with great trees and the warm land dipping southerly to the clean sea under the Marychurch cliffs.

RUDYARD KIPLING   1849

< Torquay

Torquay >

If our object in choosing to cross Devonshire by the coast road were simply to cling to the shore as closely as possible, we should, of course, follow the estuary of the Exe to Dawlish........

MRS RODOLPH STADWELL 1920's

< Dawlish Warren

Shaldon >

EXETER

The doctor's intellectual wife
Sat under the ilex tree
The Cathedral bells pealed over the wall
But never a bell heard she
And the sun played shadowgraphs on her book
Which was writ by A. Huxley.

Once those bells, those Exeter bells
Called her to praise and pray
By pink, acacia-shaded walls
Several times a day
To Wulfric's altar and riddel posts
While the choir sang Stanford in A.

The doctor jumps in his Morris car,
The surgery door goes bang,
Clash and whirr down Colleton Crescent,
Other cars all go hang
My little bus is enough for us
Till a tram-car bell went clang.

They brought him in by the big front door
And smiling corpse was he;
On the dining-room table they laid him out
Where the Bystanders used to be
The Tatler, The Sketch and The Bystander
For the canon's wives to see.

Now those bells, those Exeter bells
Call her to praise and pray
By pink, acacia-shaded walls
Several times a day
To Wulfric's altar and riddel posts
And the choir sings Stanford in A.

JOHN BETJEMAN 1937

*T*he big church made me happy - and
the fierce kings carved on the west
front - fierce persons like Gunnar and Hogni
- truculent, terrific tyrants; a contemporary
sculptor had replaced one with his notion of
a fierce king - Ruskin could write a chapter
on it, and only he could.

SIR EDWARD BURNE-JONES 1880

Exeter >

< Exeter Cathedral

The Town of Excester is a good Mile and more in cumpace, and is right strongly waullid and mainteinid. Ther be diverse fair Towers in the Toun Waul bytwixt the South and the West Gate; as the Waulles have been newly made, so have the old Towers decayed. The Castelle of Excester standith stately on a high Ground bytwixt the Est Gate and the North. Ther be 4 Gates in the Toune by the names of Est, West, North, and South; the Est and the West Gates be now the fairest and of one fascion of Building, (but) the South Gate hath beene the strongest.

JOHN LELAND   1540

"Richmond! - When last I was at Exeter,
The Mayor in courtesy showed me the castle,
And call'd it - Rouge-mont; at which name I started,
Because a bard of Ireland told me once,
I should not live long after I saw Richmond."

WILLIAM SHAKESPEARE   (RICHARD III., ACT IV. SC.II)

"I cannot leave this house without testifying to the kindness of all in it. If it is ever your ill-fortune to be ill at an inn, be sure it is the New London."

ROBERT LOUIS STEVENSON   1885

<Exeter

Exeter>

Deep-wooded combes, clear-mounded hills of morn,
Red sunset tides against a red sea-wall,
High lonely barrows where the curlews call,
Far moors that echo to the ringing horn,
Devon! thou spirit of all these beauties born,
All these are thine, but thou art more than all:
Speech can but tell thy name, praise can but fall
Beneath the cold white sea-mist of thy scorn.

HENRY NEWBOLT   1884

< Topsham

Exmouth >

Mr Duke,

I wrote to Mr Prideaux to move you for the purchase of Hayes, a farm some time in my father's possession. I will most willingly give you whatever in your conscience you shall deem it worth, and if you shall at any time have occasion to use me you shall find me a thankful friend to you and yours. I have dealt with Mr Sprint for such things as he hath at Colyton and thereabouts and he hath promised me to depart with the moiety of Otterton unto you in consideration of Hayes according to the value, and you shall not find me an ill neighbour unto you hereafter. I am resolved if I cannot entreat you to build at Colyton, but for the natural disposition I have to that place being born in that house I had rather seat myself there than anywhere else. Thus leaving the matter at large unto Mr Sprint I take my leave resting ready to countervail all your courtesies to the uttermost of my power.

Court the xxvi of June 1584

Your very willing friend in all I shall be able

SIR WALTER RALEGH

Broadhembury>

<Beehive Cottage

A couple of old border collies sprawled asleep in the road outside the post office and cabbage whites danced around the valerian sprouting from walls which had been built during the Civil War. Some of the day's heat was sandwiched between the buildings. Up ahead a farm worker drove three cows followed by a collie and a lame mongrel. The swifts screamed high against wisps of cirrus, so tiny and far off they might have strayed in from childhood summers. The absence of double yellow lines on the road helped create the illusion of timelessness.

BRIAN CARTER   1984

Mrs Boehm wrote a poem
On the Sidmouth air;
Mr Boehm read the poem
And built a cottage there.
Mr Bacon, all forsaken,
Wandered to the spot;
Mrs Bacon he has taken
Partner of his lot;
As they longer live the stronger
Their affection grows,
Every season they with reason
Bless the spot they chose!

ANON   C 1815

Sidmouth >

< Sidmouth

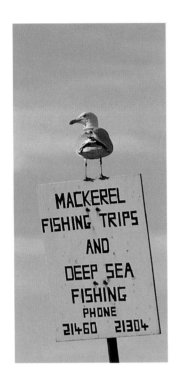

THE OTTER AND THE AXE

"Dear native brook! Wild streamlet of the West!

How many various fated years have past,

What happy and what mourneful hours, since last

I skimmed the smooth thin stone along thy breast,

Numbering its light leaps! yet so deep imprest

Sink the sweet scenes of childhood, that mine eyes

I never shut amid the sunny ray,

But straight with all their tints thy waters rise,

Thy crossing plank, thy marge with willows grey,

And bedded sand, that, veined with various dyes,

Gleamed through thy bright transparence! On my way,

Visions of childhood! oft have ye beguiled

Lone manhood's cares, yet waking fondest sighs:

Ah! that once more I were a careless child!"

SAMUEL TAYLOR COLERIDGE   C 1820

Beer >

< Beer

*O*nly last year on the well-known hill of Langridge Ford I came across a car, containing a Glasgow tradesman and his family, hopelessly stranded in the double corkscrew. Every workmen in the vicinity had rushed to the spot to offer help and, above all, advice (does not every true child of Devon prefer any job to his own and "telling" to any job whatsoever?), but after an hour of talk and endeavour the hapless man was still no further on his way to Glasgow.

SIR JOHN FORTESCUE   1932

< Axmouth

Country Lane >

Half and hour later a couple of ploughmen, who caused me the trouble of beating a new path across the field they were furrowing, made an offer also of their cider-keg. So rarely did strangers come "drow and auver" - through and over - that the sight of one kindled their hospitable feelings. They, too, had the same story to tell about dear bread, and the difficulty of providing for a family out of nine shillings a week; yet with somewhat of resignation in their tone, the result, perhaps, of long endurance. The patience of the agricultural labourer is indeed wonderful! He gets but little sympathy, has the worst seat at church, the most uncomfortable railway-carriage, and yet he, and such as he, will put on a red jacket, go away to the East or anywhere else, fight like a lion, and win a "soldiers' victory." Is it not an opprobrium to our civilization that a man, willing and able to work, should be expected to content himself and feed a wife and family with eighteenpence a day?

WALTER WHITE   1855

It was a lovely spring day when I arrived at Colby Abbey station. I had been enchanted by the countryside which I had glimpsed through the windows of the train - lush green meadows and wooded hills and the rich red soil of Devonshire with the occasional glimpse of the sea.

VICTORIA HOLT   1984

Farm Landscape >

< Hedgerow

From a position upon swelling hillsides above the valley of a river, she scanned a spacious scene, made small her eyes to focus the distance and so pursued a survey of meadow and woodland, yet without finding what she sought. Beneath and beyond, separated from her standpoint by grass lands and a hedge of hazel, tangled thickets of blackthorn, of bracken, and of briar sank to the valley bottom. Therein wound tinkling Teign through the gorges of Fingle to the sea; and above it, where the land climbed upward on the other side, spread the Park of Whiddon, with expanses of sweet, stone-scattered herbage, with tracts of deep fern, coverts of oak, and occasional habitations for the deer.

EDEN PHILLPOTTS   1899

He entered the heart of the sleeping wood. Here the trunks rose, smooth and massive for a full seventy feet before the first great boughs flared suddenly from the central columns. Beneath the roof of interlocked branches the floor of the wood was smooth and free of undergrowth; the indistinct shape of the old man blew across the spaces between the trees like a dead leaf. Tod loved this part of the wood, and feared it, too.

DAVID ROOK   1970

Fingle Bridge >

< Gnarled Tree

Oh Dartmoor! still undeemed of, and alone,
For thee what hand hath touched the powerful string?
Few know thy attributes, few tempt thy zone,
Or from thy dells one minstrel floweret bring!

I claim thee as mine own - and I may well
From early right, and long attachment claim
For thou hast oft inspired the artless shell
That breathed its spirit in no path of fame.

And I have stood beside some dark-browed rock,
And seen therefrom the stainless waters flow
Spread their live crystal o'er each jutting block,
And streak with emerald sod their tracks below.

SOPHIE DIXON   1829

< Dartmoor Sheep

Haytor >

74

It has been shrewdly said of the inhabitants of this parish (Brent Tor) that they make weekly atonement for their sins: for they can never go to church without the previous penance of climbing up this steep, which they are so often obliged to attempt with the weariest industry, and in the lowliest attitude. In windy or rainy weather, the worthy pastor himself is frequently obliged to humble himself upon all fours, preparatory to his being exalted in the pulpit.

RICHARD POLWHELE   1800

< Brent Tor

Brent Tor >

*S*uddenly, in a fearful and lamentable manner, a weighty thundering was heard, the rattling whereof did answer much like unto the sound and report of many great cannons, and terrible strange lightning therewith, greatly amazing those that heard and saw it, the darkness increasing yet more, so that they could not see one another; the extraordinary lightning came into the church so flaming, that the whole church was presently filled with fire and smoke......which so affrighted the whole congregation, that the most part of them fell down into their seats, and some upon their knees, some on their faces, and some one upon another, with a great cry of burning and scalding, they all giving themselves up for dead, supposing the last judgment day was come and that they had been in the very flames of hell.

ANON   1638

Enormous drifts fell at Ashburton during the blizzard, and most of the roads were completely blocked. At Holne Turn, half a mile from the town, there was an enormous drift a quarter of a mile in extent, and varying in height from eight to twenty feet.

ANON   1891

< Widecombe

Widecombe >

"It is a wonderful place, the moor," said he, looking round over the undulating downs, long green rollers, with crests of jagged granite foaming up into fantastic surges. "You never tire of the moor. You cannot think the wonderful secrets which it contains. It is so vast, and so barren, and so mysterious."

SIR ARTHUR CONAN DOYLE   1901

<Conversation

West Dartmoor>

Along the grassy banks how sweet to stray,
When the mild eve smiles in the glowing west,
And lengthen'd shades proclaim departing day,
And fainting sunbeams in the waters play,
When every bird seeks its accustom'd rest!
How grand to see the burning orb descend,
And the grave sky wrapp'd in its nightly robes,
Whether resplendent with the starry globes,
Or silver'd by the mildly-solemn moon;
When nightingales their lovely song resume,
And folly's sons their babbling noise suspend.

ANNE BATTEN CRISTALL 1795

River of Dart! beside thy stream
In the sweet Devon summer I linger and dream;
For thy mystic pools are dark and deep,
And thy flying waters strangely clear,
And the crags are wild by the Lover's Leap,
And thy song of sorrow I will not hear,
While the fierce moor-falcon floats aloft,
And I gaze on eyes that are loving and soft.

MORTIMER COLLINS

<Autumn Trees

River Dart>

My dear Holmes,

My previous letters and telegrams have kept you pretty well up-to-date as to all that has occurred in this most Godforsaken corner of the world. The longer one stays here the more does the spirit of the moor sink into one's soul, its vastness, and also its grim charm. When you are once out upon its bosom you have left all traces of modern England behind you, but on the other hand you are conscious everywhere of the homes and the work of the prehistoric people. On all sides of you as you walk are the houses of these forgotten folk, with their graves and huge monoliths which are supposed to have marked their temples. As you look at their grey stone huts against the scarred hillsides you leave your own age behind you, and if you were to see a skin-clad, hairy man crawl out from the low door, fitting a flint-tipped arrow on to the string of his bow, you would feel that his presence there was more natural than your own.

SIR ARTHUR CONAN DOYLE   1901

I was out on the moor, a lone place of granite rocks, tors, wind, and grey sky. The wind blew direct from the west. The great, vast, salt ocean wind. And when the wind blows over Dartmoor Forest it grasps and bends the wayfarer as easily as a blade of grass is bent. It does not blow in gusts. It blows with a great and steady determination to sweep all before it. It gives no breathing-space or quarter. A thing of power and fury, coming from immense wastes which harbour the storm devils - places vaster than any mortal man has ever conceived.

Benet's Cross >

<Grey Wethers

R THURSTON HOPKINS   1926

Dartmoor! thou wert to me, in childhood's hour,

A wild and wond'rous region. Day by day

Arose upon my youthful eye thy belt

Of hills mysterious, shadowy........

                    I feel

The influence of that impressive calm

Which rests upon them. Nothing that has life

Is visible: - no solitary flock

At will wide ranging through the silent Moor

Breaks the deep-felt monotony; and all

Is motionless save where the giant shades,

Flung by the passing cloud, glide slowly o'er

The grey and gloomy wild.

CARRINGTON

Nowhere have I experienced such a strong feeling of the ancient pastthan on Dartmoor. An atmosphere of powerful historical associations lies brooding among the stone circles, haunting the lonely menhirs,cairns and crosses that are scattered across the moor. Even the tors at times appear like mediaeval fortresses, their ramparts swarming with the fluorescent orange and blue tunics of twentieth-century walkers, come rain or shine.

Clapper Bridge>

<Dartmoor Stream

DAVID BELLAMY   1993

Devon! Devon! Devon! How much that word means! Devon! dear, sleepy old Devon! What memories that little word recalls! Some happy, some sad, for I feel that I know Devon well, and counties are like women - we only really begin to love them when we have gone through joy and sorrow and adversity with them.

Indian sages declare that the saying aloud of certain words has certain effects upon the human body. Does not saying "Devon" aloud make one feel peaceful and contented and full of old, old songs? I think so.

R THURSTON HOPKINS   1926

<Devon Fields

Devon Lane>

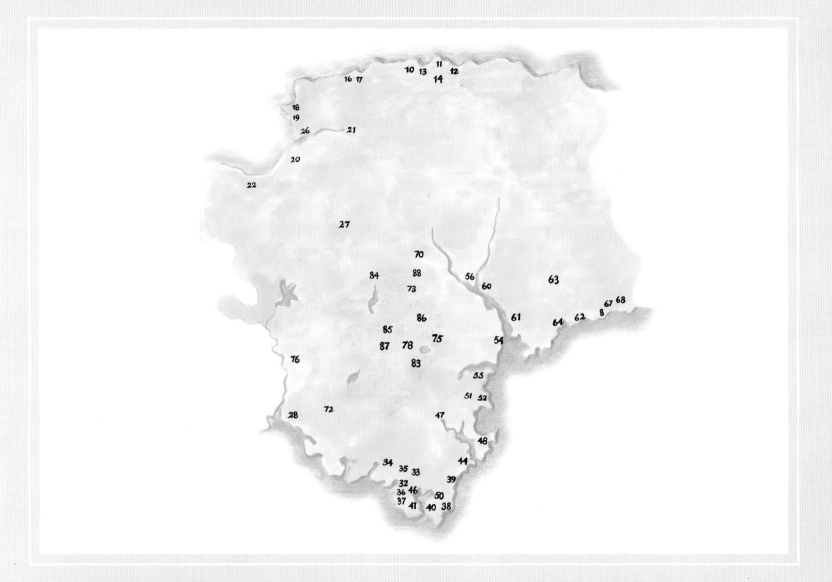

INDEX

This index contains fuller details than the photo captions, in page order.
The numbers on the map are the page numbers of the locations.

handsome old houses bear witness to the town's important and historic past.

45 BAYARD'S COVE, DARTMOUTH
From here the *MAYFLOWER* & *SPEEDWELL* sailed for the New World in 1620. When the unreliable and leaking *SPEEDWELL* reached Plymouth it was decided to continue in one ship. Now lobster pots await collection at season's end.

46 HOPE COTTAGES
Thatched cottages, in sunny corners, are typical of Devon charm.

47 TOTNES
The bridge, across the main street, in this old town was recently destroyed by fire. The replacement is a replica. Once a busting port, ships laden with timber still unload at the quay.

48 & 49 BRIXHAM NIGHT
Once the centre of England's trawler fleet, Brixham now attracts artists and tourists to the historic harbour.

50 SOUTH DEVON LANDSCAPE
Although Torbay appears to be a built-up metropolis green fields are never far away.

51 COCKINGTON
Autumn twilight shows Cockington's picturesque beauty which make it a favourite Devon village. Although almost surrounded by suburban Torquay it retains its old world charm.

52 & 53 TORQUAY
Torquay, in the heart of "The English Riviera" developed as a tourist resort with the coming of the railways in 1848. It is a sheltered spot. Not only for the many sub-tropical plants which grow in many public places but also as a haven for boats of all sizes.

54 DAWLISH WARREN
The distinct shape of the sand bar at Dawlish Warren can be clearly seen from this aerial view. Nearly 200 species of birds visit this nature reserve.

55 SHALDON
The golden glow of an early morning sunrise. The Ness towers over Shaldon at the mouth of the river Teign.

56 EXETER CATHEDRAL
The 13th century building of Exeter Cathedral is a magnificent unified structure, replacing an earlier cathedral church of which the twin Norman towers remain. Intricate carved figures on the west front provide rich decoration.

57 OLD DOORWAY
Facing towards Exeter Cathedral this doorway is a beautiful example of old craftsmanship.

58 EXETER
At the corner of the cathedral green this fine, mostly timbered, building was, for many years, a coffee house.

59 OLD EXETER
The steps of Sheepcote Hill lead down to a corner of fine, old buildings.

60 TOPSHAM
Topsham is a large village which was once a busy port, vying with Exeter for trade from the prosperous wool trade. The Countess of Devon blocked access to Exeter by building a weir. This gave her port of Topsham a big advantage. In 1566 England's first canal since Roman times was built to give Exeter access to the sea once more. The legal battle between the City of Exeter and the Countess's heirs lasted over 300 years.

61 EXMOUTH
Popular since the 18th century as a bathing resort there are some elegant houses and parks in the town.

62 BEEHIVE COTTAGE
What could be more typical of Devon's charm than a thatched cottage, flowers round the door and a post-box set into the old stone and cob wall? This cottage is at Branscombe in East Devon.

63 BROADHEMBURY
One of Devon's unspoilt villages, where time seems to have stood still.

64 & 65 SIDMOUTH
Fishing boats, hauled onto the beach, lie waiting for the tide at one end of Sidmouth's Esplanade. With red cliffs on either side the town was fashionable in Georgian and Regency times.

67 BEER
Beer was once a notorious smuggling cove. Now fishermen winch their boats onto the shingle beach.

68 AXMOUTH
Once a busy port before landslips blocked the River Axe, this tiny village has many attractive cottages.

69 COUNTRY LANE
Rolling green fields, a narrow lane and a wooden gate are everyone's idea of Devon countryside.

70 HEDGEROW TREE
A pretty hedgerow in early summer, leads to a beautiful lone tree. The purple digitalis is a common feature of Devonshire hedgerows.

71 FARM LANDSCAPE
The scars of ancient cultivation and old trackways blend with more modern tree planting and grazing to make the richness of the farming landscape.

72 GNARLED TREE
Mosses and lichens and years of weathering add character to an old tree. The river Plym at Shaugh Bridge.

73 FINGLE BRIDGE
The sheltered valleys of Dartmoor nearly all have a stream, or river, splashing through the shade of gnarled, and twisted, oak trees. Fingle Bridge is also typical of many other river crossings.

74 DARTMOOR SHEEP
Grazing freely over many thousands of acres of moorland, these hardy sheep, withstand the rigours of Dartmoor.

75 HAYTOR SUNSET
The stark, rugged beauty of Dartmoor is typified by the granite outcrops of Hay Tor.

76 BRENT TOR
The church of St. Michael stands on Brent Tor and is seen here against a dramatic sunset.

78 WIDECOMBE WINTER
Dartmoor's famous church in stark silhouette as winter snow blankets the moors.

79 WIDECOMBE
Known as the "Cathedral of the Moor" the parish church stands tall in a sheltered valley.

80 CONVERSATION!
These sheep await the shearer on one of the first hot days of summer.

81 WEST DARTMOOR
Autumn's early morning mist turns a small village into a place of mystery.

82 AUTUMN TREES
Away from the exposed moorlands, in the vale of the River Dart, trees grow straight and true.

83 RIVER DART
Autumn floods turn the River Dart into a torrent near Holne Bridge.

84 GREY WETHERS
On a high and empty part of Dartmoor lie a pair of megalithic stone circles known as Grey Wethers. Many stories relate to the sale of the stones to unsuspecting farmers, thinking they were sheep!

85 BENET'S CROSS
Numerous old stone crosses can be found on Dartmoor. Benet's Cross is at the roadside near the Warren Inn.

86 DARTMOOR STREAM
In spring the soft green shade of a small wood frames a stream above Becky Falls.

87 CLAPPER BRIDGE
This broken clapper bridge near Bellever probably dates from medieval times.

88 DEVON FIELDS
In winter hedgerow trees stand out in silhouette against the green fields of grass.

89 DEVON COUNTRY LANE
A narrow lane with high hedges and occasional oak trees.

THE WRITERS

HENRY of AVRANCHES

ELIZABETH BARRET BROWNING

DAVID BELLAMY

JOHN BETJEMAN

BOSWELL

SIR EDWARD BURNE-JONES

CARRINGTON

BRIAN CARTER

AGATHA CHRISTIE

SAMUEL TAYLOR COLERIDGE

MORTIMER COLLINS

SIR ARTHUR CONAN DOYLE

SIR AUBREY DE VERE

DANIEL DEFOE

CHARLES DICKENS

SOPHIE DIXON

REV WILLIAM EVERITT

DANIEL FARSON

SIR JOHN FORTESCUE

W HARDING THOMPSON

CHARLES G HARPER

MIRZA ABUL HASSAN KHAN

JOHN M HAWKER

VICTORIA HOLT

JOHN KEATS

CHARLES KINGSLEY

RUDYARD KIPLING

JOHN LELAND

HENRY NEWBOLT

SEAN O'CASEY

NOEL PATON

EDEN PHILLPOTTS

RICHARD POLWHELE

JOHN PRESLAND

MISS C RADFORD

SIR WALTER RALEGH

DAVID ROOK

ROBERT SOUTHEY

MRS RODOLPH STADWELL

JAN STEWER

E V THOMPSON

R THURSTON HOPKINS

RICHARD WARNER

WALTER WHITE

W H K WRIGHT

HENRY WILLIAMSON

PHOTOGRAPHER'S NOTES

It seems to be a tradition among publishers of books such as this to include a page of "technical" notes written by the photographer. I am bored by talk of cameras, lenses and films so will spare you a page of mostly useless information.

Photography is about seeing, and to see with an original and creative eye is about intuition. I rarely go out with a predetermined idea. With landscape photography I have to take the light and the view as I find them. In theory, any photographer, standing on the same spot as I stand, will produce the same photograph. In practice we all see different things and point our cameras in different directions. We also choose to do this at different times of the day. I could never put in words all the factors that make me take a photograph in a particular way but it certainly has a lot to do with how I feel about the subject in front of me.

Technique is a matter of individual preferences. I am only interested in results. However, I here offer a few guiding principles of my landscape photography.

1/ My essential equipment includes an alarm clock to wake up early and a compass to find where the sun is going to be. I also have a small double pointed quartz crystal which sits in my camera bag with the exposed film and helps to increase sharpness.

2/ The best light occurs when I am stuck in the office.

3/ If you wait for perfect conditions someone will park a truck in the view.

4/ The most I have waited in the rain for conditions to improve was five days. The picture wasn't worth waiting for and isn't in this book.

5/ Having walked for miles for a good picture I often find the best photo is right next to my car. The only problem being that I've parked right in the middle of the view.

6/ The pictures which require the most perspiration to take are always the ones that look the easiest, when you see the results.

7/ Don't run out of film.

8/ Photography is fairly easy, but it is nearly impossible to earn a living from landscape photography.

Some of these photographs were taken for the "ATMOSPHERE" range of postcards which I launched eleven years ago. The collection has been added to every year. From the outset I attempted to show what others shied away from. My first range of postcards had no blue sky in any of the photographs. To be original is difficult.

Thirty five years ago I had the good luck to be taught by Ralph Hattersley. In one year he sowed the seeds of photographic creativity which I still use today.

ACKNOWLEDGMENTS

Thanks to Julie for her invaluable help on this book.

Graham Nash and Caroline Bryant deserve thanks for processing my film over the span of my photographic career. Thirty years of perfect results is a rare record.

Thanks to Barry Pearson for his flying help with the aerial views.

No compiler or researcher of anthologies can work without the efforts of previous researchers. Credit is due to Jack Simmons for his book *A DEVON ANTHOLOGY* and to S H Burton for his book *A WEST COUNTRY ANTHOLOGY*. Much time was spent in the reference libraries in Barnstaple, Exeter and Plymouth. The Cornwall library service were also helpful in obtaining some rare books and manuscripts.

The quotation from WESTCOUNTRY by E V Thompson is reproduced with permission of E V Thompson.
The quotation from TARKA THE OTTER by Henry Williamson is reproduced by kind permission of The Henry Williamson Literary Estate.
The quotations from CHILDREN IN THE MIST (1899)/ MY DEVON YEAR (1904) by Eden Phillpotts are reproduced with permission of Aitken, Stone &Wylie Ltd.
The quotation from A PERSIAN KING AT THE COURT OF KING GEORGE 1809-10 edited and translated by Margaret Morris Cloake is reproduced with permission of Barrie & Jenkins Publishers.
The quotation from THE WILD PLACES OF BRITAIN by David Bellamy c.1986. is reproduced with permission of Michael Joseph Ltd.
The quotations from THE MOON IN THE WEIR by Brian Carter are reproduced with permission of J M Dent Publishers.
The quotation from TIME OF THE HUNTER'S MOON by Victoria Holt is reproduced with permission of A M Heath & Co Ltd.
The quotation from COLLECTED POEMS by John Betjeman is reproduced by permission of John Murray Ltd.
The quotations from BALLAD OF THE BELSTONE FOX by David Rook are reproduced by permission of Hodder & Stoughton\New England Library Ltd.
The quotation from A WINDOW ON THE SEA by Daniel Farson is reproduced by permission of A M Heath Co Ltd.
The quotations from SUNSET AND EVENING STAR by Sean O'Casey are reproduced by permission of Macmillan London Ltd.
The quotation from THE REGATTA MYSTERY by Agatha Christie Mallowan c.1936 is reproduced with permission of Hughes Massie Ltd.

Every effort has been made to contact all the copyright-holders. Should the publishers have made any mistakes in attribution we will be pleased to make the necessary arrangements at the first opportunity.